DATE DUE

GETTING TO KNOW
THE U.S. PRESIDENTS

J O H N
TYLER

TENTH PRESIDENT
1841 – 1845

WRITTEN AND ILLUSTRATED BY MIKE VENEZIA

CHILDREN'S PRESS®
A DIVISION OF SCHOLASTIC INC.
NEW YORK   TORONTO   LONDON   AUCKLAND   SYDNEY
MEXICO CITY   NEW DELHI   HONG KONG
DANBURY, CONNECTICUT

Reading Consultant: Nanci R. Vargus, Ed.D., Assistant Professor, School of Education, University of Indianapolis

Historical Consultant: Marc J. Selverstone, Ph.D., Assistant Professor, Miller Center of Public Affairs, University of Virginia

Photographs © 2005: Art Resource, NY: 3 (National Portrait Gallery, Smithsonian Institution, Washington D.C.), 14 (The New York Public Library); Bridgeman Art Library International Ltd., London/New York: 29 (Bonhams, London, UK), 18 (Museum of Fine Arts, Boston Massachusetts, USA/Gift of Martha C. Karolik for the M. and M. Karolik Collection of American Paintings, 1815-65), 16 (Museum of the City of New York, USA), 9 (New-York Historical Society, New York, USA); College of William and Mary/University Archives, Earl Gregg Swem Library: 8; Corbis Images: 28, 32; North Wind Picture Archives: 31; PictureHistory.com: 10; 23, 27, 30; Stock Montage, Inc.: 20 top right, 20 top left; Superstock, Inc.: 20 bottom.

Colorist for illustrations: Dave Ludwig

Library of Congress Cataloging-in-Publication Data

Venezia, Mike.
    John Tyler / written and illustrated by Mike Venezia.
        p. cm. — (Getting to know the U.S. presidents)
    Includes bibliographical references and index.
    ISBN 0-516-22615-0 (lib. bdg.)   0-516-27484-8 (pbk.)
    1. Tyler, John, 1790-1862—Juvenile literature. 2. Presidents—United
States—Biography—Juvenile literature. I. Title.
    E397.V46 2004
    973.5'8'0973—dc22
                                            2004000321

A portrait of John Tyler by George Healy (National Portrait Gallery, Washington, D.C.)

John Tyler was the tenth president of the United States. He was born on March 29, 1790, in Charles City County, Virginia. John Tyler was William Henry Harrison's vice president. In 1841, President Harrison died unexpectedly. No president had ever died in office before, and no one knew quite what to do. No one, that is, except John Tyler.

In 1788, two years before John Tyler was born, the U.S. Constitution was approved. It was a set of rules written to help run the new country. The Constitution was unclear, though, about what to do if a president dies. Some people thought the vice president should just take care of things for a while until the next real president was elected.

John Tyler didn't agree. He insisted that he should become the president immediately. That would show people that the United States was continuing to run smoothly. Everyone could relax knowing there was someone in charge at all times. This was probably John Tyler's most important decision.

John Tyler was the sixth child of a wealthy plantation family. When John was only seven, his mother died. His father, Judge John Tyler, was left to raise John and his seven brothers and sisters.

John was a very polite and kind boy, but he could stand up for himself when he had to. There is a legend that when John was eleven years old, he had a nasty schoolmaster. Mr. McMurdo liked to swat his pupils with a stick to keep them in order. One day John decided he had had enough. He and some classmates tied up Mr. McMurdo and locked him in the closet! Surprisingly, Judge Tyler agreed with his son's actions. He told Mr. McMurdo that cruel people usually got what they deserved.

A portrait of John Tyler's father, Judge John Tyler

As John Tyler continued in school, he proved to be an excellent student. At the age of fifteen, he entered William and Mary College in nearby Williamsburg. By age seventeen, John had graduated from college and had begun learning about law from his father. In 1809, John passed his test to become a lawyer. That same year, Judge Tyler was elected governor of Virginia.

Father and son both moved to Richmond, the state's capital city. John Tyler became a very successful lawyer in Richmond. He also became more and more interested in getting involved in Virginia's government.

A painting showing Richmond, Virginia, in the early 1800s

A portrait of
Letitia Tyler

John Tyler was a talented public speaker
and very likeable. Soon, he was elected to the
Virginia legislature. The legislature is the part
of a government responsible for making laws.
During this time, John met Letitia Christian,
the daughter of another wealthy plantation
owner. John and Letitia dated for five years
before they got married.

Like many parents of the time, Letitia's parents were very strict. They never left the couple alone until John and Letitia were married. John Tyler didn't even kiss Letitia's hand until three weeks before the wedding!

In 1813, when John and Letitia got married, the United States was in the middle of fighting a war. The War of 1812 was the nation's second war with Great Britain.

John Tyler had learned all about the first war with Britain, the Revolutionary War, from stories his father had told. John didn't care for the way Britain had once ruled the American colonies. He decided to help his country fight the British again. Even though John didn't know anything about being a soldier, he joined a volunteer army group.

Surprisingly, John was made a captain.
Once, in the middle of the night, John and
his troops were warned that the British were
coming. Captain Tyler and his men were in
such a hurry to fight that they toppled down
a flight of stairs and ended up in a big pile.
Luckily, it was only a false alarm.

A painting showing a street in Washington, D.C., in 1817

Fortunately for Captain John Tyler, the war soon ended. John went back to being a lawyer and got more interested in running for government jobs. In 1816, he was elected to the U.S. House of Representatives. John traveled to Washington, D.C. He was surprised to find the capital of the United States in such a mess.

In 1816, the streets of Washington were all muddy, with pigs and cows walking through them! When John was invited to have dinner with President Madison and his wife Dolley, it was at a temporary home. The White House was being repaired because it had been badly damaged during the War of 1812.

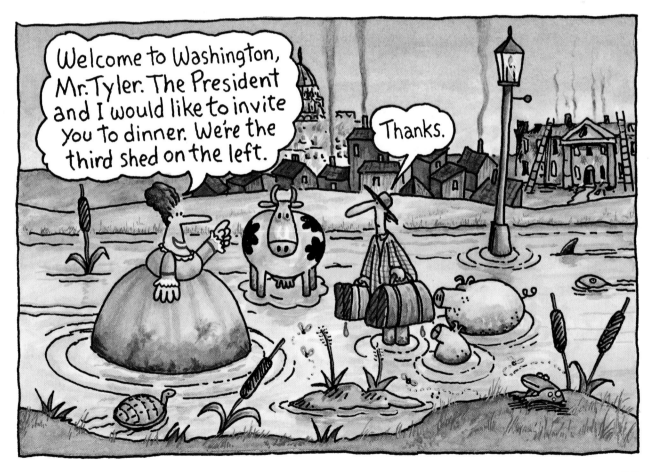

In the early 1800s, many people who lived in big northern cities such as New York (above) wanted a strong federal government that would help big cities grow and prosper.

As a young member of Congress, John Tyler fought hard for what he believed in. Even though it was years before the Civil War began, John could see that the northern and southern states were in danger of splitting apart. These states were always arguing about what was best for them.

Many people in the North wanted a stronger central government to control all the states. They thought federal money should be spent on roads and canals to connect the states. Cities and industries were growing fast in the North, and people there wanted a government that would help them. Most northerners also agreed that slavery was wrong and should be stopped.

Southerners used slaves to run their plantations in the early 1800s (above). Like most southerners at that time, John Tyler believed each state should get to decide for itself whether to allow slavery.

People in the southern states had different ideas. They lived mainly on farms and in small towns. They definitely wanted to keep slaves to help run their cotton and tobacco plantations.

Most southerners wanted the federal government to stay out of their business. They also felt each state should be responsible for raising its own money to build roads and canals.

Being from the southern state of Virginia, John Tyler agreed that states should have more power to govern themselves. He also believed in slavery. John Tyler owned slaves his whole adult life. Most of his time in Congress was spent trying to convince northern Congressmen that the South should be able to run things its way.

Daniel Webster

John Calhoun

Henry Clay

While John Tyler was representing his state, three great Americans were in Congress at the same time. Over the years, John would have many dealings with Daniel Webster, Henry Clay, and John Calhoun. These three men were excellent speakers who were great at expressing fresh, important ideas.

Even though it was an exciting time, John Tyler left his job before his term was up. After eating some spoiled fish, Tyler became seriously ill and decided to return home. John often had troublesome stomach problems. Even so, some people felt that the real reason he resigned his position was that he thought too many members of Congress were ignoring his ideas.

John Tyler didn't stay away from politics for long, though. He ended up becoming governor of Virginia and then a U.S. senator. In 1834, he joined a new political party, called the Whigs, that was being formed by Henry Clay, Daniel Webster, and John Calhoun.

The WHIGS in 1840

HARRISON AND TYLER

The WHIGS in 1776

AND REFORM!
In the Expenses of the Government.

A campaign handkerchief from the 1840 presidential election

A political party is a group that supports politicians who agree with its views. Today there are two main political parties, the Republicans and the Democrats. In John Tyler's time, there were the Whigs and the Democrats. In 1840, the Whigs asked John Tyler to run as vice president along with their presidential candidate, William Henry Harrison.

After a very exciting presidential race, William Henry Harrison and John Tyler won against President Martin Van Buren. At that time, being vice president wasn't a very important job. Vice presidents led the meetings of the U.S. Senate. They also attended parties, dances, and dinners. John Tyler was expecting the next four years to be pretty peaceful and quiet.

Then something happened that would change John Tyler's life forever. After only a month in office, President Harrison died! He caught a cold that turned into pneumonia. Everyone was shocked, especially John Tyler. Vice President Tyler left his home in Virginia immediately and traveled to Washington, D.C.

When Vice President Tyler arrived in Washington, he made his most important decision. He claimed all the rights and privileges of the presidency. He took the oath of office, moved into the White House, and made a presidential speech. Many people were upset and angered. John Tyler had suddenly become president of the United States without anyone voting for him!

At first, President Tyler's Whig friends were happy. They thought they could count on President Tyler to listen to their ideas just as President Harrison had. President Tyler surprised everyone, though. He decided to listen to no one and do what he thought was right, even if it made more people angry.

A portrait of John Tyler as president by James Reid Lambdin

In spite of making quite a few enemies, John Tyler did get some important things done as president. He controlled his opponents in Congress by using his veto power. After Congress passes a bill, the president has to sign it for it to become law. The president can refuse to sign, or veto, the bill. Then the bill can become law only if Congress can get two-thirds of the members there that day to vote for the bill. Overriding a president's veto can be hard. President Tyler used his veto power often.

This 1844 political cartoon, which shows Tyler as a donkey, makes fun of how often the president vetoed bills sent to him by Congress.

President Tyler opened the door for the United States to trade with China. This painting shows U.S. ships and other ships in the port of Canton, China, in the mid-1800s.

President Tyler sent explorers to check out the Oregon Territory, the farthest northwest region of the country. He also started trading goods with China and helped Britain and the United States finally agree on the exact boundaries between certain states and Canada.

Julia Gardiner Tyler was John Tyler's second wife.

One very sad thing happened during John Tyler's presidency. In 1842, his wife Letitia died. A few months later, John met and fell in love with Julia Gardiner. When they married in 1844, Tyler became the first U.S. president to get married while in office.

President Tyler decided not to run for a second term as president. In 1842, the Whigs had kicked him out of their party. They were tired of the president being so stubborn and vetoing their ideas. The Democrats didn't like President Tyler very much, either. Without the support of a political party, John Tyler felt he would never have a chance to be reelected. One of the last things John Tyler did as president was arrange to make Texas a state.

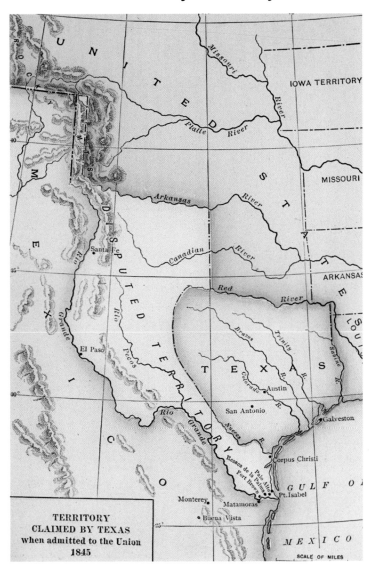

TERRITORY
CLAIMED BY TEXAS
when admitted to the Union
1845

This map shows how Texas looked when it was admitted as a state in 1845.

A photograph of John Tyler

In 1845, John Tyler returned to his home in Virginia. He worked hard to find a way to keep the United States from splitting apart, but there was little he could do. As the states prepared for civil war, John Tyler was chosen to be a member of the new Confederate government.

John Tyler died in 1862, about ten months after the Civil War began. Luckily, he never saw the destruction of the southern states he loved so much.